Acknowledgements

With thanks for the inspiration and guidance from my whizz-kidz advisors: George, Milo, Chloe, Sophie, Rebecca, Katie, Jimmy, David and Nathan.

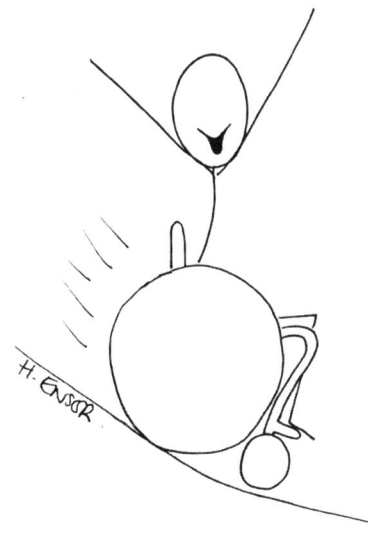

For more books written and
illustrated by
Hannah Ensor, see

www.stickmancommunications.co.uk

*First edition published 2011
2QT Limited (Publishing)
Burton In Kendal
Cumbria LA6 1NJ
www.2qt.co.uk

Cover design and Illustrations by
Hannah Ensor
The author has her own website:
www.stickmancommunications.co.uk

Printed in Malta on behalf of Latitude Press Limited

A CIP catalogue record for this book is available
from the British Library
ISBN 978-1-908098-32-0

All web addresses and contact details correct at time of printing

Biscuit Baking

Written and illustrated by Hannah Ensor

Produced in association with Whizz-kidz

Choosing tasty
things to bake.

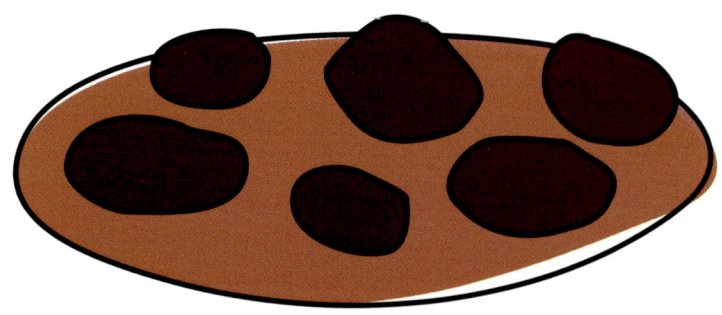

Measuring the sugar and weighing out the butter.

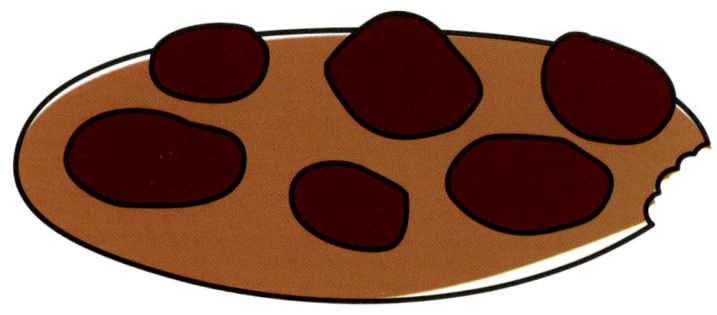

Glooping in the
syrup,

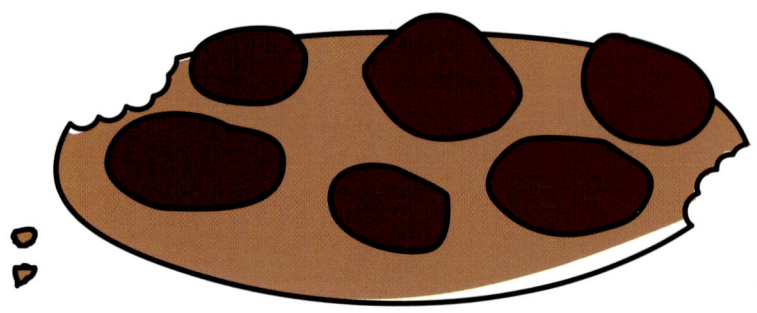

and pouring in
the flour.

"1 cup of chocolate drops"...

...and maybe a few more.

Mix it up all yummy
scrummy.

Daddy says "don't
eat it yet!"

Ooops!

Squish it into
biscuit shapes,

and bake it in the oven.

£1 from the sale of each book will be donated to Whizz-Kidz to help more children enjoy fun and full childhoods, and get the right wheelchairs for them at the right time.

Whizz-Kidz Registered charity number 802872.

www.whizz-kidz.org.uk

Whizz-Kidz,
4th floor,
Portland House,
Bressenden Place,
London,
SW1E 5BH.